Daniel in the Lions' Den

Daniel 1-2, 4-6

Retold by Pamela Broughton
Illustrated by Tom LaPadula

A GOLDEN BOOK • NEW YORK

Western Publishing Company, Inc., Racine, Wisconsin 53404

In the days when Nebuchadnezzar was king of
Babylon, the lands of Israel and Babylon were at war.
Finally, after a great battle, Nebuchadnezzar
conquered Israel and captured its great city,
Jerusalem.

Nebuchadnezzar ordered an officer to bring a number of Israelite boys back to Babylon. Among those taken was a boy named Daniel.

Each day, as the king had commanded, the boys were served the choicest food and wine.

But Daniel asked permission to eat only vegetables and drink only water. He did not want to eat the king's food, because doing so was against God's law.

God caused the king's officer to look kindly on Daniel. After that, Daniel did not have to eat the king's food.

God was pleased with Daniel for obeying His law. He gave Daniel wisdom and the ability to understand dreams.

At the end of three years Daniel and three of his friends were chosen to serve the king.

The king found Daniel and his friends wiser than all the magicians, sorcerers, and wise men in the kingdom.

Nebuchadnezzar had dreams that troubled him and kept him from sleeping. He sent for his magicians, sorcerers, and wise men.

The king wanted the wise men to tell him what his dreams meant. But the wise men could not do it.

Nebuchadnezzar became angry. He ordered his soldiers to kill all the wise men in the kingdom. Then the soldiers began their search for the wise men. And they went to find Daniel and his friends to kill them as well.

But Daniel persuaded the officer in charge to let him talk with the king.

Daniel said to the king, "If you will wait till tomorrow, I will tell you not only the meaning of your dream, I will tell you *what* you dreamed!"

Nebuchadnezzar agreed.

Daniel went home, and he and his friends prayed
to God.

That night God showed Daniel the king's dream in
a vision.

The next day Daniel told the king what he had dreamed and what the dream meant. The king bowed to Daniel and honored him.

Then Nebuchadnezzar said, "Surely your God is the God of gods, since He caused you to be able to explain this mystery."

Nebuchadnezzar made Daniel governor over Babylon and chief of all the wise men. Daniel's three friends were appointed to help him rule.

The king had another dream, and he sent for
Daniel. When Daniel heard Nebuchadnezzar's dream,
he was frightened. But the king told Daniel to say
what the dream meant.

So Daniel said, "You will be driven away from your
people. You will live with the animals and eat grass
like the cattle. Seven years will pass. Then you will
recognize that God rules—even over kings."

One year later Nebuchadnezzar was looking out over Babylon and thinking how great his city was.

A voice from heaven said, "Your kingdom has been taken away from you. You will be driven away from your people."

All that Daniel had told the king immediately came true. Nebuchadnezzar was driven away from his palace. He lived with the animals and ate grass like the cattle. His hair grew like eagles' feathers and his nails like birds' claws.

So Nebuchadnezzar lived for seven years. But after the seven years had passed, he praised and honored God. Then he became king once more.

Nebuchadnezzar soon died. His son, Belshazzar, became king. But Belshazzar did not honor God.

One day Belshazzar gave a banquet. A hand suddenly appeared and began writing on the wall in front of him. All the guests were frightened, but none of them could read the writing.

Then the queen remembered Daniel, and Belshazzar sent for him.

Daniel said Belshazzar had not served God, as his father had learned to do. Then he read the writing on the wall. He said, "God has put an end to your kingdom. It has been given to your enemies."

That very night Belshazzar was killed, and Darius the Mede became king. Darius appointed Daniel and two other men to govern the kingdom.

Darius soon found that Daniel was a better governor than the others. Darius wished to appoint Daniel to govern the entire kingdom by himself.

That made the other governors angry. They tricked Darius into making a new law: Any person who prayed to anyone but the king would be thrown into a den of lions.

Daniel knew about the new law. But he still prayed to God three times a day, as was his custom.

The other governors found Daniel praying. They
told Darius that Daniel had broken the law. And they
said that Daniel should be thrown into the lions' den.

Darius was sorry. He tried to think of a way to
rescue Daniel, but he could not.

So Daniel was brought inside the lions' den. A large stone was rolled across the opening to seal him in.

Darius could not sleep all night. He rose at dawn and ran to the lions' den. He called out to Daniel, "Has your God been able to save you?"

Daniel answered, "My God sent his angels and shut the lions' mouths."

The stone was rolled away from the opening, and Daniel walked out. Darius was overjoyed. He commanded that the other governors be thrown into the lions' den. And he ordered all the people of his kingdom to worship the living God of Daniel, who had delivered his servant from the power of the lions.